# ASSESSING PERSISTENT AND EMERGING CYBER THREATS TO THE U.S. IN THE HOMELAND

## JOINT HEARING

BEFORE THE

## SUBCOMMITTEE ON COUNTERTERRORISM AND INTELLIGENCE

AND THE

## SUBCOMMITTEE ON CYBERSECURITY, INFRASTRUCTURE PROTECTION, AND SECURITY TECHNOLOGIES

OF THE

## COMMITTEE ON HOMELAND SECURITY HOUSE OF REPRESENTATIVES

ONE HUNDRED THIRTEENTH CONGRESS

SECOND SESSION

MAY 21, 2014

## Serial No. 113–69

Printed for the use of the Committee on Homeland Security

Available via the World Wide Web: http://www.gpo.gov/fdsys/

U.S. GOVERNMENT PRINTING OFFICE

89–764 PDF        WASHINGTON : 2014

For sale by the Superintendent of Documents, U.S. Government Printing Office
Internet: bookstore.gpo.gov   Phone: toll free (866) 512–1800; DC area (202) 512–1800
Fax: (202) 512–2250   Mail: Stop SSOP, Washington, DC 20402–0001

## COMMITTEE ON HOMELAND SECURITY

MICHAEL T. MCCAUL, Texas, *Chairman*

LAMAR SMITH, Texas
PETER T. KING, New York
MIKE ROGERS, Alabama
PAUL C. BROUN, Georgia
CANDICE S. MILLER, Michigan, *Vice Chair*
PATRICK MEEHAN, Pennsylvania
JEFF DUNCAN, South Carolina
TOM MARINO, Pennsylvania
JASON CHAFFETZ, Utah
STEVEN M. PALAZZO, Mississippi
LOU BARLETTA, Pennsylvania
RICHARD HUDSON, North Carolina
STEVE DAINES, Montana
SUSAN W. BROOKS, Indiana
SCOTT PERRY, Pennsylvania
MARK SANFORD, South Carolina
VACANCY

BENNIE G. THOMPSON, Mississippi
LORETTA SANCHEZ, California
SHEILA JACKSON LEE, Texas
YVETTE D. CLARKE, New York
BRIAN HIGGINS, New York
CEDRIC L. RICHMOND, Louisiana
WILLIAM R. KEATING, Massachusetts
RON BARBER, Arizona
DONDALD M. PAYNE, JR., New Jersey
BETO O'ROURKE, Texas
FILEMON VELA, Texas
ERIC SWALWELL, California
VACANCY
VACANCY

BRENDAN P. SHIELDS, *Staff Director*
MICHAEL GEFFROY, *Deputy Staff Director/Chief Counsel*
MICHAEL S. TWINCHEK, *Chief Clerk*
I. LANIER AVANT, *Minority Subcommittee Staff Director*

---

## SUBCOMMITTEE ON COUNTERTERRORISM AND INTELLIGENCE

PETER T. KING, New York, *Chairman*

PAUL C. BROUN, Georgia
PATRICK MEEHAN, Pennsylvania, *Vice Chair*
JASON CHAFFETZ, Utah
VACANCY
MICHAEL T. MCCAUL, Texas *(ex officio)*

BRIAN HIGGINS, New York
LORETTA SANCHEZ, California
WILLIAM R. KEATING, Massachusetts
BENNIE G. THOMPSON, Mississippi *(ex officio)*

MANDY BOWERS, *Subcommittee Staff Director*
DENNIS TERRY, *Subcommittee Clerk*
HOPE GOINS, *Minority Subcommittee Staff Director*

---

## SUBCOMMITTEE ON CYBERSECURITY, INFRASTRUCTURE PROTECTION, AND SECURITY TECHNOLOGIES

PATRICK MEEHAN, Pennsylvania, *Chairman*

MIKE ROGERS, Alabama
TOM MARINO, Pennsylvania
JASON CHAFFETZ, Utah
STEVE DAINES, Montana
SCOTT PERRY, Pennsylvania, *Vice Chair*
MICHAEL T. MCCAUL, Texas *(ex officio)*

YVETTE D. CLARKE, New York
WILLIAM R. KEATING, Massachusetts
FILEMON VELA, Texas
VACANCY
BENNIE G. THOMPSON, Mississippi *(ex officio)*

ALEX MANNING, *Subcommittee Staff Director*
DENNIS TERRY, *Subcommittee Clerk*

(II)

# CONTENTS

# ASSESSING PERSISTENT AND EMERGING CYBER THREATS TO THE U.S. IN THE HOMELAND

---

**Wednesday, May 21, 2014**

U.S. House of Representatives,
Committee on Homeland Security,
Subcommittee on Counterterrorism and
Intelligence, and
Subcommittee on Cybersecurity, Infrastructure
Protection, and Security Technologies,
Washington, DC.

The subcommittees met, pursuant to call, at 10:04 a.m., in Room 311, Cannon House Office Building, Hon. Peter T. King [Chairman of the Subcommittee on Counterterrorism and Intelligence] presiding.

Present: Representatives King, Broun, Meehan, Perry, Clarke, Higgins, and Vela.

Mr. KING. Good morning. The Committee on Homeland Security, Subcommittee on Counterterrorism and Intelligence, and the Subcommittee—chaired by Mr. Meehan—on Cybersecurity, Infrastructure Protection, and Security Technologies will come to order.

The subcommittees are meeting today to hear testimony examining persistent and emerging cyber threats to the United States. It is particularly fortuitous or appropriate that we hold this hearing in view of the fact that just the other day the Justice Department announced indictments of several Chinese Army officials for their role in violating cybersecurity. Again, this hearing had been scheduled for several weeks. Ranking Member Higgins and I have been working on this for quite a while now. But again I think the fact that we are holding it this week is particularly appropriate.

Due to the sensitivity of today's hearing, the subcommittees will enter a closed portion with the witnesses to discuss Classified and sensitive matters, and I ask unanimous consent that at the appropriate time the subcommittees recess and reconvene in closed session in the committee's secure space. Without objection, so ordered.

I will now recognize myself for an opening statement.

The expanding number of cyber actors, ranging from nation-states to terrorists to criminals, as well as increasing attack capability and the increasing intensity of cyber attacks around the globe, have made cyber warfare and cyber crime one of the most significant threats facing the United States. This week the Department of Justice unsealed an indictment against five Chinese individuals working for the Chinese military for hacking into multiple private-sector U.S. businesses to steal their sensitive proprietary

(1)

information. Additionally, this week the FBI and international law enforcement arrested over 100 people for using malicious software called Blackshades, which is used remotely to take over a computer, turn on the web cam, and access passwords and other information without the owner's knowledge.

I am encouraged by the DOJ indictment and the recent law enforcement operation. I hope it is a signal of more aggressive U.S. actions to address the cyber threat as we move forward, because this threat is not going away. Cyber attacks have economic consequences, harm our National security, and could be used to carry out attacks on the U.S. homeland.

Over the last decade the threats facing the United States have become more diverse, as have the tools for conducting attacks and waging war. While the United States has made great strides to secure the homeland since 9/11, our enemies have evolved, and we must now consider that a foreign adversary, terrorist network, or a criminal organization will use cyberspace to penetrate America's defenses.

Director of National Intelligence James Clapper featured the cyber threat prominently in his annual threat update to Congress this year. Along with other U.S. officials, he painted a sobering picture of the potential fallout from a cyber attack.

Nation-states comprise the most capable cyber actors around the globe. Countries such as Russia, China, and Iran have demonstrated a willingness to use cyber space to steal our military secrets, target our critical infrastructure, and even attack our free press and financial sector. Each has invested a great deal in cyber defenses and offensive capabilities, and some have even used cyber attacks as a proxy in a physical military confrontation. Many experts have suggested that Russian actors engaged in offensive attacks in Estonia to support military forces during their 2008 invasion of Georgia and again during the recent annexation of Crimea.

In addition to the threat from foreign powers, American citizens and companies lose billions from organized cyber crime every year. Traditional criminal networks have wasted no time in developing their on-line tradecraft to scam, steal, and destroy valuable data. The recent data breach at Target is a great example of exactly how far-reaching and sophisticated these operations are. Department of Homeland Security plays a major role in helping private companies keep their networks secure, and this will only become more important in years to come.

Finally, we are accustomed to think of the physical damage caused by terrorist networks to life and property. We must now be prepared to defend against groups like al-Qaeda using increasingly sophisticated cyber attacks and cyber crimes to their advantage. For many years we have also seen these groups and violent Islamist extremists use the internet to communicate, radicalize, and spread their hate.

Today we will hear about these issues from witnesses provided by the FBI and DHS. I am pleased that we will begin this hearing in an open session and subsequently move into a closed, executive session.

I am particularly pleased that Chairman Pat Meehan is here today and that his subcommittee is engaged in this hearing, because he, along with Chairman McCaul, have led this committee's efforts to enact serious cybersecurity legislation. With the support of the private sector and privacy advocates, their bill was passed unanimously out of this committee. It is a testament to their hard work; also to the importance of the issues. I am really privileged to have Pat working with us here today.

I welcome those on the front line of the issue and I look forward to their testimony.

I now recognize the Ranking Minority Member of the Subcommittee on Counterterrorism and Intelligence, the gentleman from New York, Mr. Higgins, for any statement he may have.

Mr. HIGGINS. I would like to thank the Chairman for holding this hearing, and in deference to the Chairman and our guests today, I will submit my opening statement for the record so we can get right to it.

[The statement of Mr. Higgins follows:]

STATEMENT OF RANKING MEMBER BRIAN HIGGINS

MAY 21, 2014

I would like to thank the Chairman for holding today's hearing. I look forward to hearing the testimony of our witnesses as the committee continues to expand our interests and understanding of the current and evolving cyber threats. I have gone on record before to state that cyber threats know no limits and have no boundaries. As a Member representing the Buffalo and Niagara region, I dedicate a significant amount of my time and interests to issues related to border security and the facilitation of commerce.

However, I understand the threats to our country and our way of life are not limited to the reach of planes, trains, and automobiles, and also that these threats cannot be contained by Congressional districts. As technology continues to mature and our on-line world continues to grow, the threats and the means to carry out those threats grow as well. For the second consecutive year, the director of national intelligence, James Clapper has designated cybersecurity as the top global threat. Also, the No. 2 global threat for the United States on this same list is related to concerns of espionage.

As a reflection of the growing espionage cyber threats, on Monday, for the first time in U.S. history, the Department of Justice issued indictments related to cybersecurity against foreign state actors. Pursuant to that indictment, five members of the Chinese military were charged with a total of 155 counts of crimes related to computer hacking, economic espionage, and other offenses related to cybersecurity. I believe this indictment sends a strong message for state-actors that the United States will not be intimidated by cyber hackers and we will remain vigilant against attempts against cyber espionage. While I understand that the unprecedented nature of this indictment has and will continue to interest Members of this committee and Congress as a whole, I will refrain from interfering with the on-going judicial process.

However, I would request that as information can be shared with us, our witnesses will return to brief Members of this committee in the appropriate setting. America's economic prosperity depends on cybersecurity, and that is why we need effective oversight and robust cyber legislation that includes strategic initiatives, including public-private partnerships that protect our Nation from hackers, nefarious state actors, and foreign intelligence services from countries such as China.

While I understand that it would be inappropriate for our witnesses to go into detail about specific cyber threats in this open setting; when possible, I believe an open discussion of the threats that we do know about, the technologies being used, and massive vulnerabilities can be helpful to the American public. It is clear to everyone that our dependence on technology is growing exponentially by the day.

Therefore our Nation depends on us, both Congress and Federal agencies and departments, to have a robust, comprehensive set of cybersecurity policies and procedures in place. Therefore, we must not only examine the threat, but also protect critical infrastructure and safeguard our personal and financial information, while promoting research and development to ensure that we have the proper protocols in place.

Mr. KING. The Ranking Member yields back.

Chairman Meehan.

Mr. MEEHAN. I thank the Ranking Member for yielding, and I thank the Chairman for sharing the opportunity to collaborate on, as Chairman King said, this very, very important issue. I want to thank everybody for attending this important hearing.

This is the latest in a series of hearings the Subcommittee on Cybersecurity, Infrastructure Protection, and Security Technologies has held examining the threat to our computer networks and what the U.S. Government is doing to mitigate and respond to that threat. The threat of cyber attack is real, and it is a growing menace in American security and prosperity. Over the past year alone we have seen Iranian hackers disrupt the computer systems of Saudi energy company Aramco in an attempt to take down the American financial sector. We have also seen criminals attack some of the icons of our retail sector, compromising the personal information of over 100 million customers. Just this week the Department of Justice announced indictments against five Chinese military operatives for hacking into U.S. companies to steal proprietary information.

Last month I had the opportunity to travel to China with a number of my colleagues, including House Majority Leader Eric Cantor, and we met with a number of China's most senior leaders, up to and including the Premier, and we specifically raised concerns about state-sponsored industrial espionage and the importance of protecting and respecting intellectual property and the trade secrets of American businesses. China has a responsibility to adhere to international law, a responsibility it has repeatedly failed to acknowledge.

The response we received from Chinese officials where we raised these concerns was disciplined. The Chinese refused to admit that they condoned or supported their state-sponsored corporate espionage, and they refused to concede that American businesses were routinely targeted by Chinese hackers for intrusion.

In addition to state-sponsored and criminal organizations, ideologically motivated actors, including terrorist groups and activists, use the internet to attack us and to finance their illicit activities. As the 2014 report by the cybersecurity firm Mandiant states, threat actors are not just interested in seizing the corporate crown jewels, but are also looking for ways to publicize their views, to cause physical destruction, and to influence global decision makers.

Defending against and responding to these attacks has a real cost, and the cost is primarily borne by the American private sector. Companies spend hundreds of millions of dollars per year defending their networks. At a hearing we held last month in Philadelphia, just an area community bank testified that they had to spend a million dollars a year—this is a small community bank—on its cybersecurity efforts, and they suggested they could spend much more.

Attacks that cause business disruptions cost companies an average of nearly $300,000 each to mitigate the damage, and certainly it can be significantly higher where there is real damage, and companies that have lost untold amounts of intellectual property have found themselves at a competitive disadvantage with their global competitors. Identity theft alone costs U.S. banks, retailers, and consumers roughly $780 million a year, and as the Chairman himself said, literally billions of dollars in value associated with stolen intellectual property.

All of these losses directly contribute to job losses, missed business opportunities, and American companies at a competitive disadvantage on the world stage. The question then becomes: How do we respond to this?

First, we must ensure that our Federal agencies have defined roles and are coordinating with each other and the private sector to share threat information. We must also crack down on the perpetrators of these attacks by arresting malicious hackers and pressuring other countries to do the same. It is especially true in China and Eastern Europe, where these companies' spies and criminals hide.

The indictments of the Chinese military hackers and the arrest of over 100 hackers linked to the malicious software called Blackshades are a good start, but there is more work to do. Importantly, we in Congress need to continue to study this threat and to understand who the adversaries are, what they want, where they live, and what they are capable of doing.

I want to thank each of the members of this panel who are before us today for their work in this area, and we look forward to your testimony both in here and in the closed hearings to better understand and to better continue to educate not only our colleagues, but the American people on this very, very important and challenging issue. I thank Chairman King for the opportunity to share it with him.

I yield back.

Mr. KING. Thank you, Chairman Meehan.

Other Members of the committee are reminded that opening statements may be submitted for the record.

[The statement of Mr. Thompson follows:]

STATEMENT OF RANKING MEMBER BENNIE G. THOMPSON

MAY 21, 2014

This hearing is timed only days after the Department of Justice announced indictments against five Chinese military officials for conducting cyber espionage against U.S. industries related to nuclear power and solar and metal products. I understand the investigative role of the FBI in this investigation and that our judicial process limits the information which can be shared at such a critical point in this process. Therefore, I look forward to working with all of our witnesses to discuss and review this case at the appropriate time.

During this Congress and in previous Congresses, I have maintained and expanded this committee's cybersecurity jurisdiction by conducting effective oversight and offering both responsive and responsible legislation. I continue to be encouraged as DHS assumes its role as the primary agency charged with securing Federal Government systems from cyber attacks, while working with other agencies to collect information, analyze threats, and respond accordingly.

It is important for DHS to continue to make progress in addressing one of the greatest homeland security challenges of our day—how to help Government agencies and private-sector infrastructure owners and operators protect critical infrastructure from cyber threats.

Too often when we discuss cyber threats or cybersecurity, we group all bad actors into the same category. Today, our witnesses should explain not only the on-going threats, but also distinguish the threat actors. Specifically, I am interested in hearing about the organized crime groups and their efforts to target financial service sectors, terrorist groups' use of on-line networks to recruit and organize attack efforts, and foreign governments with an interest in obtaining data and information from Government agencies and major manufacturers, including those with defense contracts.

I would also like to hear how the witnesses and their agencies manage and analyze the volumes of open-source information and postings that can be found on various social networking websites.

I have gone on record several times to emphasize social media as an integral tool in recognizing and preventing emerging threats, but warning that a balance must be created to manage this information. We must still heed that warning and make our Federal security regime as effective as possible.

Mr. KING. Now I am pleased to introduce the distinguished panel that we have here today.

Mr. Glenn Lemons is the senior intelligence officer for the Cyber Intelligence Analysis Division in Homeland Security's Office of Intelligence and Analysis. His responsibilities include providing all-source cyber intelligence support for DHS senior personnel and owners and operators of critical infrastructure. Additionally, he manages and leads a diverse cyber workforce that, in coordination with the National Protection and Programs Directorate, provides operational intelligence support to our Nation's 16 critical infrastructure partners and all applicable State, local, territorial, Tribal, and private-sector entities.

Mr. Joseph Demarest is the assistant director of the Cyber Division at the Federal Bureau of Investigation. The FBI helps lead the National effort to investigate high-tech crimes, including cyber-based terrorism, espionage, computer intrusions, and cyber fraud. Joe Demarest has been with the FBI for more than a quarter of a century, and I had the personal privilege of seeing him operate first-hand when he headed the Joint Terrorism Task Force in New York and later as the assistant director in charge, where he did a truly outstanding job in coordinating efforts against terrorism in the New York City, Long Island, New York area.

So, Joe Demarest, it is great to see you here today. Thank you.

Larry Zelvin is the director of National Cybersecurity and Communications Integration Center at the Department of Homeland Security—easier to say NCCIC. It is comprised of several components, including the U.S. Computer Emergency Readiness Team, the National Coordination Center for Telecommunications, the Industrial Control Systems Cyber Emergency Response Team, and a 24/7 operations center. Mr. Zelvin is a retired U.S. Navy captain and naval aviator with 26 years of active service.

I want to thank all of you for appearing here today, and let you know that your written testimony is being submitted for the record. I will now recognize Mr. Lemons for 5 minutes for his testimony.

Mr. Lemons.

## STATEMENT OF GLENN LEMONS, SENIOR INTELLIGENCE OFFICER, CYBER INTELLIGENCE ANALYSIS DIVISION, OFFICE OF INTELLIGENCE AND ANALYSIS, U.S. DEPARTMENT OF HOMELAND SECURITY

Mr. LEMONS. Thank you, sir.

Chairman King, Chairman Meehan, Ranking Member Higgins, and distinguished Members of the committee, I am pleased to be here today to discuss the continued threat to the homeland from malicious cyber actors and the Office of Intelligence and Analysis role in assessing these threats.

Cyber intrusions into critical infrastructure and Government networks are increasing in sophistication and seriousness. Although the persistent cyber threat to the homeland remains theft of data and espionage, the complexity of emerging threat capabilities, the inextricable link between physical and cyber domains, and a diversity of cyber actors present challenges to DHS and all of our customers.

With the private sector owning and operating over 85 percent of our Nation's critical infrastructure, information sharing becomes especially important between public and private sector. Malicious cyber actors who target the homeland include nation-states, cyber criminals, criminal hackers, asymmetric actors, to include terrorists, with the insidious and/or unwitting insider presenting unique cybersecurity concerns that can magnify any threat.

Nation-states aggressively target and gain persistent access to public and private-sector networks to exploit and steal massive quantities of data. Given the increasing world view of cyber space as a domain of warfare, we cannot discount that adversaries currently support planning for contingencies by mapping and evaluating U.S. networks and infrastructure. Cyber criminals are largely motivated by profit and are extremely capable, representing a long-term global and common threat. We see sophisticated financial criminals in many countries throughout the world.

Criminal hackers are politically or ideologically motivated and target for publicity, which can result in high-profile operations in both, but often with limited effectiveness. The May 2000 Middle East and North Africa-based hacker campaign known as OpUSA showed the group's desire for media attention, despite its lack of capability to disrupt websites of U.S. Government, financial, and commercial entities.

Asymmetrical actors, to include terrorists, primarily use the internet for on-line recruitment, communication, propaganda, and research. While limited by persistent counterterrorism pressures and difficulty in recruiting experts, we believe they will continue to seek cyber targets of opportunity. Therefore, despite the low probability of a destructive terrorist cyber attack occurring, such an event may have a high-profile impact, even if unsuccessful. Success in this case may be determined by press coverage by its destructive network activity.

The outlook of these threats is that malicious cyber activity targeting Government and private-sector networks can result in intentional and in some cases unintentional consequences which can threaten National and economic security, critical infrastructure, as well as public health and welfare. It is reasonable to assess both disruptive and possibly destructive cyber activity are the goals of malicious cyber actors who target our Nation's critical infrastructure in an effort to cause harm.

I&A has an important role in supporting the Department in carrying out its cyber responsibilities by assessing these emerging threats and ensuring both public and private sector are made aware of them through robust information sharing. The I&A support for public and private-sector owners and operators is multidimensional. Since the implementation of Executive Order 13636, which charges the Department to increase the value, the quantity, and quality of Unclassified cyber threat reporting, DHS I&A has increased Unclassified cyber outreach by 382 percent from fiscal year 2012 to 2013, and for 2014 we are on a trajectory to bypass last year's numbers. These activities are in addition to our regularly scheduled Unclassified and Classified production, and weekly, monthly, and quarterly security engagements.

Additionally, we are partnering with State and local fusion centers to deconflict production, solicit requirements, and participate in joint production opportunities. These are just some of our efforts to increase threat awareness, decrease duplicative reporting, and align priorities.

Thank you for providing me the opportunity to speak with you today about these important issues. I look forward to your questions both here and in the follow-on Classified session.

Mr. KING. Thank you for your testimony, Mr. Lemons.

Now I am pleased to recognize Mr. Demarest.

## STATEMENT OF JOSEPH DEMAREST, ASSISTANT DIRECTOR, CYBER DIVISION, FEDERAL BUREAU OF INVESTIGATION

Mr. DEMAREST. Good morning, Chairmen King, Meehan, and Ranking Member Higgins, and distinguished Members. I am pleased to appear before you today to discuss the cyber threats facing our Nation and how the FBI and our partners, most importantly DHS and a broadband of others domestically and abroad, what we are doing together to protect the United States.

Today's FBI is a threat-focused, intelligence-driven organization. Just as our adversaries continue to evolve, so, too, must the FBI. We live in a time of acute and persistent terrorist, state-sponsored, and criminal threats to our National security, our economy, and our communities. These diverse threats facing our Nation and our neighborhoods underscore the complexity and breadth of the FBI's mission today.

The United States faces cyber threats from state-sponsored hackers, hackers for hire, global cyber criminal syndicates, and terrorists. They seek our trade and state secrets, our technology, our personal and financial information, and our ideas, all of which are of incredible value to us here in the United States. Given the scope of the cyber threat, agencies across the Federal Government are making cybersecurity obviously a top priority. Within the FBI we are prioritizing high-level intrusions. The biggest and most dangerous botnets, criminal forums, state-sponsored hackers, and global cyber criminal syndicates are our priorities. We want to predict and prevent attacks and get to the position where we can, rather than simply react to after the fact.

FBI agents, analysts, and computer scientists are using technological capabilities and traditional investigative techniques to fight cyber crime today. We are working side-by-side with our Federal, State, and local partners on cyber task forces in each of our 56 field offices and through the National Cyber Investigative Joint Task Force in Chantilly, Virginia. Through our 24/7 cyber command center, CyWatch, we combine the resources of the FBI and the NCIJTF, allowing us to provide connectivity to the other Federal cyber centers, NCCIC being chief among them, Government agencies, FBI field offices, legal attachés, and the private sector in the event of a cyber event.

As the committee is well aware, the frequency and impact of cyber attacks on our Nation's private sector and Government networks have increased dramatically in the past decade and are expected to grow exponentially. The FBI and our partners have had multiple recent investigative successes against the threat and we are continuing to push ourselves to respond more rapidly to prevent attacks before they occur.

On Monday the Western District of Pennsylvania unsealed an indictment naming five members of the People's Liberation Army of the People's Republic of China on 31 counts, including conspiring to commit computer fraud, accessing a computer without authorization for the purpose of commercial advantage and private financial gain, damaging computers through the transmission of code and commands, aggravated identity theft, economic espionage, and theft of trade secrets. Each of the defendants provided his individual expertise to a conspiracy to penetrate the computer networks of six U.S. companies while those companies were engaged in negotiations or joint ventures with or were pursuing legal action against state-owned enterprises in China. This marks the first time criminal charges have been filed against known state actors for hacking.

Also on Monday the FBI announced a world-wide operation against those individuals who created and purchased malware known as Blackshades. This operation involved 18 countries. More than 90 arrests have been made so far, and more than 300 searches have been conducted around the world in support of the operation. Blackshades products were offered on their website. Their products include Blackshades Remote Access Tool and Blackshades Password Recovery, to name just a few.

The most popular product was the Blackshades Remote Access Tool. The tool contained a key logger feature that allowed users to record each key the victim typed on their computer keyboards. To help users steal a victim's password and other log-on credentials, the tool also had a form-grabber feature which automatically captured log-on information that victims entered into the forms on their infected computers. The tool also provided its users with complete access to all the files contained on a victim's computer. A tool user could use this access to view or download photographs, documents, or other files on the victim's computer. Further, the tool enabled users to encrypt or lock a victim's files and demand ransom payment to unlock them, much like ransomware. The tool even came with a prepared script to demand such a ransom. As you can imagine, this tool alone poses a significant threat to individual victims across the United States and certainly around the world.

These successes are just the beginning. The FBI has redoubled its efforts to strengthen our cyber capabilities internally. The FBI's Next Generation Cyber Initiative, which we launched in 2012, included a wide range of developments, like establishing the cyber task forces throughout each of our field offices; also focusing on cyber intrusion or intrusion investigations. We have also hired additional computer scientists to assist in the technical investigations in the field and at headquarters; and then certainly expanded our partnerships to enhance collaboration through the NCIJTF and within the U.S. Government.

The NCIJTF, which serves as a coordination, integration, and information-sharing center among 19 U.S. agencies and our Five Eyes partners for cyber threat investigations has provided unprecedented coordination. This coordination involves senior personnel at key agencies. NCIJTF, which is led by the FBI, has deputy directors from the NSA, DHS, CIA, U.S. Secret Service, and U.S. Cyber Command.

In addition to strengthening our partnerships in Government and law enforcement, we recognize that to effectively combat the cyber threat we must significantly enhance our cooperation with the private sector, which we are doing through our InfraGard program; our DSAC program as well. We recognize that understanding the cyber threat is critical to effectively combatting that, and the private sector is a key ingredient. As part of our enhanced private-sector outreach, we have begun to provide industry partners with Classified threat briefings and indicators in advance of attacks that we are knowledgeable of.

In conclusion, sir, to counter the threats we face today, we are engaging in an unprecedented level of collaboration within the U.S. Government, with the private sector, and with our international partners. We are grateful for the committee's continued support and look forward to working with you and expanding our partnerships as we determine a successful course forward for this Nation to defeat the cyber adversaries we face today. Thank you again, sir.

[The prepared statement of Mr. Demarest follows:]

PREPARED STATEMENT OF JOSEPH DEMAREST

MAY 21, 2014

Good morning Chairmen Meehan and King and Ranking Members Clarke and Higgins. I'm pleased to appear before you today to discuss the cyber threats facing our Nation and how the FBI and our partners are working together to protect the United States Government and private-sector networks.

Today's FBI is a threat-focused, intelligence-driven organization. Each employee of the FBI understands the key threats facing our Nation and we must constantly strive to be more efficient and more effective. Just as our adversaries continue to evolve, so, too, must the FBI. We live in a time of acute and persistent terrorist, state-sponsored, and criminal threats to our National security, our economy, and our communities. These diverse threats facing our Nation and our neighborhoods underscore the complexity and breadth of the FBI's mission.

We remain focused on defending the United States against terrorism, foreign intelligence, and cyber threats; upholding and enforcing the criminal laws of the United States; protecting civil rights and civil liberties; and providing leadership and criminal justice services to Federal, State, local, and international agencies and partners.

THE CYBER THREAT & FBI RESPONSE

The United States faces cyber threats from state-sponsored hackers, hackers for hire, global cyber syndicates, and terrorists. They seek our state secrets, our trade secrets, our technology, our personal and financial information, and our ideas, all of which are of incredible value to all of us. They may seek to strike our critical infrastructure and our economy.

Given the scope of the cyber threat, agencies across the Federal Government are making cybersecurity a top priority. Within the FBI, we are prioritizing high-level intrusions—the biggest and most dangerous botnets, state-sponsored hackers, and global cyber syndicates. We want to predict and prevent attacks, rather than simply react after the fact.

FBI agents, analysts, and computer scientists are using technical capabilities and traditional investigative techniques, such as sources and communication intercepts, as well as forensics, to fight cyber crime. We are working side-by-side with our Federal, State, and local partners on Cyber Task Forces in each of our 56 field offices and through the National Cyber Investigative Joint Task Force (NCIJTF). Through our 24/7 cyber command center, CyWatch, we combine the resources of the FBI and NCIJTF, allowing us to provide connectivity to Federal cyber centers, Government agencies, FBI field offices and legal attachés, and the private sector in the event of a cyber intrusion.

We also work with the private sector through partnerships such as the Domestic Security Alliance Council, InfraGard, and the National Cyber Forensics and Training Alliance. The FBI is training our State and local counterparts to triage local cyber matters, so that we can focus on the most pressing issues with National impact.

In addition, our Legal Attaché offices overseas work to coordinate cyber investigations and address jurisdictional hurdles and differences in the law from country to country. We are supporting partners at Interpol and The Hague as they work to establish international cyber crime centers. We continue to assess other locations to ensure that our cyber personnel are in the most appropriate locations across the globe.

We know that to be successful in the fight against cyber crime, we must continue to recruit, develop, and retain a highly-skilled workforce. To that end, we have developed a number of creative staffing programs and collaborative partnerships with private industry to ensure that over the long term we remain focused on our most vital resource, our people.

As the committee is well aware, the frequency and impact of cyber attacks on our Nation's private sector and Government networks have increased dramatically in the past decade and are expected to continue to grow.

RECENT SUCCESSES

While the FBI and our partners have had multiple recent investigative successes against the threat, we are continuing to push ourselves to respond more rapidly and prevent attacks before they occur.

One area in which we recently have had great success with our overseas partners is in targeting infrastructure we believe has been used in Distributed Denial of Service (DDOS) attacks, and preventing that infrastructure from being used for future attacks. A DDOS attack is an attack on a computer system or network that causes a loss of service to users, typically the loss of network connectivity and services by consuming the bandwidth of the victim network. Since October 2012, the FBI and the Department of Homeland Security (DHS) have released nearly 168,000 Internet Protocol addresses of computers that were believed to be infected with DDOS malware. We have released this information through Joint Indicator Bulletins (JIBs) to more than 130 countries via DHS's National Cybersecurity and Communications Integration Center (NCCIC), where our liaison officers provide expert and technical advice for increased coordination and collaboration, as well as our Legal Attachés overseas.

These actions have enabled our foreign partners to take action and reduced the effectiveness of the botnets and the DDOS attacks. We are continuing to target botnets through this strategy and others.

In April 2013, the FBI Cyber Division initiated an aggressive approach to disrupt and dismantle the most significant botnets threatening the economy and National security of the United States. This initiative, named Operation Clean Slate, was implemented to appropriately address the threat neutralization actions through collaboration with the private sector, Department of Homeland Security and other United States Government partners, and our foreign partners. This includes law enforcement action against those responsible for the creation and use of the illegal botnets, mitigation of the botnet itself, assistance to victims, public-service announcements, and long-term efforts to improve awareness of the botnet threat through community outreach. Although each botnet is unique, Operation Clean Slate's strategic approach to this significant threat ensures a comprehensive neutralization strategy, incorporating a unified public/private response and a whole-of-Government approach to protect U.S. interests.

The impact of botnets has been significant. Botnets have caused over $113 billion in losses globally, with approximately 378 million computers infected each year, equaling more than 1 million victims per day, translating to 12 victims per second.

To date, Operation Clean Slate has resulted in several successes. Working with our partners, we disrupted the Citadel Botnet. This botnet was designed to facilitate unauthorized access to computers of individuals and financial institutions to steal on-line banking credentials, credit card information, and other personally identifiable information. Citadel was responsible for the loss of over a half billion dollars. As a result of our actions, over 1,000 Citadel domains were seized, accounting for more than 11 million victim computers world-wide. In addition, working with foreign law enforcement, we arrested a major user of the malware.

Building on the success of the disruption of Citadel, in December 2013, the FBI and Europol, together with Microsoft and other industry partners, disrupted the ZeroAccess Botnet. ZeroAccess was responsible for infecting more than 2 million computers, specifically targeting search results on Google, Bing, and Yahoo search engines, and is estimated to have cost on-line advertisers $2.7 million each month.

In January 2014, Aleksandry Andreevich Panin, a Russian national, pled guilty to conspiracy to commit wire and bank fraud for his role as the primary developer and distributer of the malicious software known as "Spyeye" which infected over 1.4 million computers in the United States and abroad. Based on information received from the financial services industry, over 10,000 bank accounts were compromised by Spyeye infections in 2013 alone. Panin's co-conspirator, Hamza Bendelladj, an Algerian national who helped Panin develop and distribute the malware, was also arrested in January 2013 in Bangkok, Thailand.

### NEXT GENERATION CYBER INITIATIVE

The need to prevent attacks is a key reason the FBI has redoubled our efforts to strengthen our cyber capabilities while protecting privacy, confidentiality, and civil liberties. The FBI's Next Generation Cyber Initiative, which we launched in 2012, entails a wide range of measures, including focusing the FBI Cyber Division on intrusions into computers and networks, as opposed to crimes committed with a computer as a modality. The Cyber Division established Cyber Task Forces in each of our 56 field offices to conduct cyber intrusion investigations and respond to significant cyber incidents. The Cyber Division has also hired additional computer scientists to assist with technical investigations in the field and expanded partnerships to enhance collaboration with the NCIJTF.

The NCIJTF, which serves as a coordination, integration, and information-sharing center among 19 U.S. agencies and our Five Eyes partners for cyber threat investigations has resulted in unprecedented coordination. This coordination involves senior personnel at key agencies. NCIJTF, which is led by the FBI, now has deputy directors from the NSA, DHS, the Central Intelligence Agency, U.S. Secret Service, and U.S. Cyber Command. In the past year, we have had our Five Eyes partners join us at the NCIJTF. Australia embedded a liaison officer in May 2013, the United Kingdom in July 2013, and Canada in January 2014. By developing partnerships with these and other nations, NCIJTF is working to become the international leader in synchronizing and maximizing investigations of cyber adversaries.

While we are primarily focused with our Federal partners on cyber intrusions, we are also working with our State and local law enforcement partners to identify and address gaps in the investigation and prosecution of internet fraud crimes.

Currently, the FBI's Internet Crime Complaint Center (IC3) collects reports from private industry and citizens about on-line fraud schemes, identifies emerging trends, and produces reports about them. The FBI investigates fraud schemes that are appropriate for Federal prosecution (based on such factors as the amount of loss). Others are packaged together and referred to State and local law enforcement.

The FBI is also working to develop the Wellspring program in collaboration with the International Association of Chiefs of Police, the Major Cities Chiefs Association, and the National Sheriffs' Association to enhance the internet fraud targeting packages IC3 provides to State and local law enforcement for investigation and potential prosecution. During the first phase of this program's development, IC3 worked with the Utah Department of Public Safety to develop better investigative leads for direct dissemination to State and local agencies.

Through IC3, Operation Wellspring provided Utah police 22 referral packages involving over 800 victims, from which the FBI opened 14 investigations. Additionally, another 9 investigations were opened and developed from the information provided. The following are reported loss totals:

- IC3-referred investigations=$2,135,264.
- Cyber Task Force initiated investigations=$385,630.
- Operation Wellspring/Utah Total=$2,520,894.

The FBI is also partnering closely with DOJ's Bureau of Justice Assistance to support efforts of the International Association of Chiefs of Police to develop a National Cyber Center designed specifically to identify and share resources from across Government to assist local, State, and Tribal law enforcement agencies better address their cyber crime needs.

The FBI's newly-established Guardian for Cyber application, being developed for Cyber use by the Guardian Victim Analysis Unit (GVAU), provides a comprehensive platform that tracks U.S. Government coordination and efforts to notify victims or targets of malicious cyber activity.

The FBI is working toward the full utilization of Guardian for Cyber across FBI, other Government agencies, State, local, Tribal, and territorial (SLTT) governments, as well as industry partners, in order to provide forward understanding of cyber-related threats, increase awareness of victim actions to mitigate those threats, and facilitate a coordinated overall cyber incident response by the U.S. Government.

### PRIVATE SECTOR OUTREACH

In addition to strengthening our partnerships in Government and law enforcement, we recognize that to effectively combat the cyber threat, we must significantly enhance our collaboration with the private sector. Our Nation's companies are the primary victims of cyber intrusions and their networks contain the evidence of countless attacks. In the past, industry has provided us information about attacks that have occurred, and we have investigated the attacks, but we have not always provided information back.

The FBI's newly-established Key Partnership Engagement Unit (KPEU) manages a targeted outreach program focused on building relationships with senior executives of key private-sector corporations. Through a tiered approach the FBI is able to prioritize our efforts to better correlate potential National security threat levels with specific critical infrastructure sectors.

The KPEU team promotes the FBI's Government and industry collaborative approach to cybersecurity and investigations by developing a robust information exchange platform with its corporate partners.

Through the FBI's InfraGard program, the FBI develops partnerships and working relationships with private sector, academic, and other public/private entity subject-matter experts. Primarily geared toward the protection of critical, National infrastructure, InfraGard promotes on-going dialogue and timely communication between a current active membership base of 25,863 (as of April 2014).

InfraGard members are encouraged to share information with Government that better allows Government to prevent and address criminal and National security issues. One of the resources available to members is the Guardian for Cyber program, which facilitates real-time incident reports to the FBI. InfraGard members also benefit from access to robust on- and off-line learning resources, connectivity with other members and special interest groups, and relevant Government intelligence and information updates that enable them to broaden threat awareness and protect their assets.

The FBI's Cyber Initiative & Resource Fusion Unit (CIRFU) maximizes and develops intelligence and analytical resources received from law enforcement, academia, international, and critical corporate private-sector subject-matter experts to identify and combat significant actors involved in current and emerging cyber-related criminal and National security threats. CIRFU's core capabilities include a partnership with the National Cyber Forensics and Training Alliance (NCFTA) in Pittsburgh, Pennsylvania, where the unit is collocated. NCFTA acts as a neutral platform through which the unit develops and maintains liaison with hundreds of formal and informal working partners who share real-time threat information and best practices, and who collaborate on initiatives to target and mitigate cyber threats domestically and abroad. In addition, the FBI, Small Business Administration, and the National Institute of Standards and Technology (NIST) partner together to provide cybersecurity training and awareness to small business as well as citizens leveraging the FBI InfraGard program.

The FBI recognizes that understanding the cyber threat is critical to effectively combating it. As part of our enhanced private-sector outreach, we have begun to provide industry partners with Classified threat briefings and other information and tools to better help them repel intruders. Earlier this year, in coordination with the Treasury Department, we provided a Classified briefing on threats to the financial services industry to executives of more than 40 banks who participated via secure video teleconference in FBI field offices. We provided another Classified briefing on threats to the financial services industry in April 2014, with 100 banks participating. Another illustration of the FBI's commitment to private-sector outreach is our increase in production of our external use products such as the FBI Liaison Alert System (FLASH) reports and Private Industry Notifications (PINs).

CONCLUSION

In conclusion, to counter the threats we face, we are engaging in an unprecedented level of collaboration within the U.S. Government, with the private sector, and with international law enforcement.

We are grateful for the committee's continued support and look forward to working with you and expanding our partnerships as we determine a successful course forward for the Nation to defeat our cyber adversaries.

Mr. KING. Thank you, Mr. Demarest.

Now Mr. Zelvin.

## STATEMENT OF LARRY ZELVIN, DIRECTOR, NATIONAL CYBER-SECURITY AND COMMUNICATIONS INTEGRATION CENTER, NATIONAL PROTECTION AND PROGRAMS DIRECTORATE, U.S. DEPARTMENT OF HOMELAND SECURITY

Mr. ZELVIN. Chairman King, Chairman Meehan, Ranking Members Higgins, Ranking Member Clarke, distinguished Members of the committee, thank you for the opportunity to appear before you today.

As you well know, the Nation's economic vitality and National security depend on a secure cyber space where reasonable risk decisions can be made and the flow of digital goods, transactions, and on-line interactions can occur safely and reliably. In order to meet this objective, the technical characteristics of malicious cyber activity must be shared in a timely fashion so cyber defenders can discover, address, and mitigate a variety of threats and vulnerabilities.

In carrying out our particular responsibilities, the NCCIC promotes and implements a unified approach to cybersecurity which enables the rapid sharing of cybersecurity information in a manner that ensures the protection of individuals' privacy, civil liberties, and rights.

The NCCIC is a civilian organization that provides an around-the-clock center where Government, private sector, and international partners can work together in both physical and virtual environments. As mentioned, the NCCIC is comprised of four branches, US–CERT, ICS–CERT, NCC, and an ops and integration component.

From October 1, 2013, to May 20, 2014, the NCCIC has received over 350,000 cyber incident reports from Government partners, critical infrastructure organizations, and international partners, a significant increase from the nearly 230,000 reports received in all of fiscal year 2013. These reports included incidents such as distributed denial of service attacks, phishing campaigns, and intrusions into a variety of technology information systems.

In response to these incidents, the NCCIC regularly publishes technical and nontechnical information products, often co-authoring with the FBI, analyzing the characteristics of malicious cyber activity, improving the ability of the organizations, their ability to reduce risk. Additionally, when appropriate, all NCCIC components have on-site incident response teams that can assist asset owners and operators and their facilities, in close cooperation with our Government partners.

US–CERT's global partnerships with more than 200 other CERTs world-wide are particularly useful as our team works to develop analysis across international borders to develop a comprehensive picture of malicious cyber activity. Data from the NCCIC and US–CERT can also be shared in machine-readable formats called a Structured Threat Information eXpression language, also known as STIX, which is currently being implemented and utilized.

When looking at cyber threats, one of our greatest challenges in cybersecurity is, is our information technology systems are not nearly as secure as they could or should be. While there are a number of cases I could use to highlight my statement, I would like to use my remaining time to talk about how we in DHS aided Federal departments and agencies respond to and mitigate to the Heartbleed vulnerability across the dot-gov domain.

On April 17, 2014, the NCCIC learned of a vulnerability in the widely-used Secure Sockets Layer encryption software dubbed Heartbleed. On April 8, US–CERT issued a public alert on the Heartbleed vulnerability and deployed signatures into our EINSTEIN 2 intrusion detection system to enable the detection of possible exploitation of the Heartbleed in the dot-gov domain. On April 10, mitigation guidance was distributed to our national world-wide partners, and then the NCCIC's National Cybersecurity Assessment & Technical Services team collaborated with well over 100 Federal agencies, receiving their authorization to scan for the Heartbleed vulnerability, identify their public IP space, schedule times to conduct the scanning, and then deliver individualized reports and results to each agency for their mitigation.

To date, the NCATS team has scanned Federal IP space of approximately 15.5 million IPs on 11 different occasions and assisted reducing the number of Federal Heartbleed vulnerability occurrences from 270 to about 2 in less than 3 weeks. More than half of these vulnerabilities were identified and mitigated in the first 6 days of scanning.

The Industrial Control System CERT, in partnership with private-sector research groups, conducted two webinars regarding Heartbleed, one with the Industrial Control System vendor community on April 16 and one with 16 critical infrastructure sectors directly impacted by the vulnerability on April 25. Approximately 140 vendors attended the first session and nearly 500 critical infrastructure asset and owner-operators, as well as representatives from sector-specific agencies and information-sharing and analysis centers, attended the second.

Fortunately, due to the hard work throughout the Federal Government, the impact of the Heartbleed on the dot-gov domain has been minimal. I am very proud of how the team responded and continues to counter this significant vulnerability as it serves as yet another example of how we collaborate with and serve a large community of stakeholders. We still can do better, and we are asking for the help of the committee to clarify DHS' authorities so it can better mitigate threats to the dot-gov and our dot-com domains closer to the time in which they occur.

In conclusion, I would like to again thank the committee for the ability to appear today and highlight that we in DHS and across the NCCIC strive every day to enhance the security and resilience across cyber space and the information technology enterprise. We accomplish our mission using voluntary means and ever-mindful of the need to respect privacy, civil liberties, and the law. I truly appreciate the opportunity to speak with you today and look forward to your questions.

[The prepared statement of Mr. Zelvin follows:]

PREPARED STATEMENT OF LARRY ZELVIN

MAY 21, 2014

INTRODUCTION

Chairman King, Chairman Meehan, Ranking Member Higgins, Ranking Member Clarke, and distinguished Members of the committee, I am pleased to appear today to discuss the Department of Homeland Security (DHS) National Protection and Programs Directorate (NPPD) and the National Cybersecurity and Communications Integration Center (NCCIC) efforts to assess persistent and emerging cyber threats to the U.S. homeland.

On February 12, 2013, the President signed Executive Order (E.O.) 13636, *Improving Critical Infrastructure Cybersecurity* and Presidential Policy Directive (PPD) 21, Critical Infrastructure Security and Resilience, which set out steps to strengthen the security and resilience of the Nation's critical infrastructure, and reflect the increasing importance of integrating cybersecurity efforts with traditional critical infrastructure protection. The President also highlighted that it is important for Government to encourage efficiency, innovation, and economic prosperity while promoting safety, security, business confidentiality, privacy, and civil liberties. DHS partners closely with critical infrastructure owners and operators to improve cybersecurity information sharing and encourage risk-based implementation of standards and guidelines in order to strengthen critical infrastructure security and resilience.

In my testimony today, I would like to highlight how DHS helps secure cyber infrastructure and then discuss a few specific examples where we have prevented incidents and responded to a variety of cybersecurity challenges.

ENHANCING THE SECURITY OF CYBER INFRASTRUCTURE

Based on our statutory authorities, and in response to policy requirements, DHS coordinates the National protection, prevention, mitigation of, and recovery from significant cyber and communications incidents; disseminates domestic cyber threat and vulnerability analysis across various sectors; and investigates cyber crimes under DHS's jurisdiction. DHS has a unique responsibility in securing Federal civilian systems against all threats and hazards. DHS components actively involved in cybersecurity include NPPD, the United States Secret Service, the U.S. Coast Guard, U.S. Customs and Border Protection, Immigration and Customs Enforcement, the DHS Office of the Chief Information Officer, and the DHS Office of Intelligence and Analysis (I&A), among others. In all of its activities, DHS coordinates all of its cybersecurity efforts with public, private-sector, and international partners.

The DHS National Cybersecurity & Communications Integration Center (NCCIC) is a 24x7 cyber situational awareness and incident response and management center that serves as a centralized location where operational elements involved in cybersecurity and communications reliance coordinate and integrate cybersecurity efforts. NCCIC partners include all Federal departments and agencies; State, local, Tribal, and territorial governments (SLTT); the private sector; and international entities. NCCIC's activities include providing greater understanding of cybersecurity and communications vulnerabilities, intrusions, incidents, mitigation, and recovery actions. The NCCIC is composed of the United States Computer Emergency Readiness Team (US–CERT), the Industrial Control System Cyber Emergency Response Team (ICS–CERT), the National Coordination Center for Communications (NCC), and an Operations and Integration Team. NCCIC operations are currently conducted from three States—Virginia, Idaho, and Florida. During the first 7 months of fiscal year 2014, the NCCIC has received 31,593 reports of incidents, detected over 28,000 vulnerabilities, issued over 4,006 actionable cyber alerts, and had over 252,523 partners subscribe to our cyber threat warning sharing initiative.

The NCCIC actively collaborates with public and private-sector partners every day, including responding to and mitigating the impacts of attempted disruptions to the Nation's critical cyber and communications networks. In fiscal year 2014 so far, the Industrial Control Systems Cyber Emergency Response Team (ICS–CERT) has provided over 161 alerts, bulletins, and other products to the ICS community warning of various threats and vulnerabilities impacting control systems, tracked 85 unique vulnerabilities affecting ICS products, conducted 41 assessments across critical infrastructure sectors, and deployed the Cyber Security Evaluation Tool to 2,412 critical infrastructure owners and operators to assist in performing their own cyber-security self-assessments against known control systems standards.

DHS also directly supports Federal civilian departments and agencies in developing capabilities that will improve their own cybersecurity posture. Through the Continuous Diagnostics and Mitigation (CDM) program, led by the NPPD Federal Network Resilience Branch, DHS enables Federal agencies to more readily identify network security issues, including unauthorized and unmanaged hardware and software, known vulnerabilities, weak configuration settings, and potential insider attacks. Agencies can then prioritize mitigation actions for these issues based on potential consequences or likelihood of exploitation by adversaries. The CDM program provides diagnostic sensors, tools, and dashboards that provide situational awareness to individual agencies, as well as general situational awareness at the Federal level. Memoranda of Agreement with the CDM program encompass over 97 percent of all Federal civilian personnel.

Complementing these efforts, the National Cybersecurity Protection System (NCPS), a key component of which is referred to as EINSTEIN, is an integrated intrusion detection, analysis, information sharing, and intrusion-prevention system, utilizing hardware, software, and other components to support DHS's mandate to protect Federal civilian agency networks. In fiscal year 2014 and beyond, the program will expand intrusion prevention, information sharing, and cyber analytic capabilities at Federal agencies. EINSTEIN 3 Accelerated (E3A) currently provides Domain Name System and/or email protection services to a total of seven departments and agencies, and we are working with our service providers to bring coverage to the rest of the Executive branch. However, this process has been significantly delayed by the lack of clear authorities for DHS. E3A gives DHS an active role in defending .gov network traffic and significantly reduces the threat vectors available to malicious actors seeking to harm Federal networks.

SECURING THE HOMELAND AGAINST PERSISTENT AND EMERGING CYBER THREATS

Cyber intrusions into critical infrastructure and Government networks are serious and sophisticated threats. The complexity of emerging threat capabilities, the inextricable link between the physical and cyber domains, and the diversity of cyber actors present challenges to DHS and all of our customers. Because the private sector owns and operates a significant percentage of the Nation's critical infrastructure, information sharing becomes especially critical between the public and private sectors.

*Heartbleed*

The Department recently learned of a serious vulnerability, known as "Heartbleed," a weakness in the widely-used OpenSSL encryption software that protects the electronic traffic across two-thirds of the internet and in scores of electronic devices. Although new computer "bugs" and malware crop up almost daily, this vulnerability is unusual in how widespread it is, the potentially damaging information it allows malicious actors to obtain, and the length of time before it was discovered.

NCCIC learned of the of the Heartbleed vulnerability on April 7, 2014. Less than 24 hours later, NCCIC released alert and mitigation information on the US–CERT website. In close coordination with the Departments of Defense and Justice, as well as private-sector partners, the NCCIC then created a number of compromise detection signatures for the EINSTEIN system that were also shared with additional critical infrastructure partners. DHS worked with civilian agencies to scan their .gov websites and networks for Heartbleed vulnerabilities, and provided technical assistance for issues of concern identified through this process. The NCCIC and its components also began a highly active outreach to cyber researchers, critical infrastructure owners, operators, and vendors, Federal, and SLTT entities, and international partners to discuss measures to mitigate the vulnerability and determine if there had been active exploits.

Once in place, DHS began notifying agencies that EINSTEIN signatures had detected possible activity, and immediately provided mitigation guidance and technical assistance.

The administration's May 2011 Cybersecurity Legislative Proposal called for Congress to provide DHS with clear statutory authority to carry out this operational mission, while reinforcing the fundamental responsibilities of individual agencies to secure their networks, and preserving the policy and budgetary coordination oversight of the Office of Management and Budget and the Executive Office of the President. While there was rapid and coordinated Federal Government response to Heartbleed, the lack of clear and updated laws reflecting the roles and responsibilities of civilian network security caused unnecessary delays in the incident response.

*Point-of-Sale Compromises*

On December 19, 2013, a major retailer publically announced it had experienced unauthorized access to payment card data from the retailer's U.S. stores. The information involved in this incident included customer names, credit and debit card numbers, and the cards' expiration dates and card verification value security codes (i.e., the three- or four-digit numbers that are usually on the back of the card). Separately, another retailer reported a malware incident involving its Point-of-Sale (POS) system on January 11, 2014, that resulted in the apparent compromise of credit card and payment information.

In response to this activity, NCCIC/US–CERT analyzed the malware identified by the Secret Service as well as other relevant technical data and used those findings, in part, to create two information-sharing products. The first product, which is publically available and can be found on US–CERT's website, provides a non-technical overview of risks to POS systems, along with recommendations for how businesses and individuals can better protect themselves and mitigate their losses in the event an incident has already occurred. The second product provides more detailed technical analysis and mitigation recommendations, and has been shared through non-public, secure channels with industry partners to enable their protection efforts. When possible, NCCIC's goal is always to share information broadly, including by producing products tailored to specific audiences.

These efforts ensured that actionable details associated with a major cyber incident were shared quickly and accurately with the private-sector partners who needed the information in order to protect themselves and their customers, while also providing individuals with practical recommendations for mitigating the risk associated with the compromise of their personal information. NCCIC especially benefited from close coordination with the private-sector Financial Services Information Sharing and Analysis Center (FS–ISAC) during this response.

*Energy Sector*

In March 2012, DHS identified a campaign of cyber intrusions targeting natural gas pipeline sector companies with spear-phishing e-mails that dated back to December 2011. The attacks were highly-targeted, tightly-focused, and well-crafted.

ICS–CERT kicked off an "Action Campaign" in partnership with the Federal Bureau of Investigation, Department of Energy (DOE), Electricity Sector–Information Sharing and Analysis Centers, Transportation Security Administration, and others to provide Classified briefings to private-sector critical infrastructure organizations across the country. In May and June 2012, DHS deployed on-site assistance to two of the organizations targeted in this campaign: An energy company that operates a gas pipeline in the United States and a manufacturing company that specializes in producing materials for pipeline construction. ICS–CERT and the Federal Bureau of Investigation (FBI) provided 14 briefings in major cities throughout the United States to over 750 personnel involved in the protection of energy assets and critical infrastructure.

ICS–CERT, in coordination with DOE and the Federal Energy Regulatory Commission (FERC), has also started an initiative dubbed "SAFEGUARD" to assess the cybersecurity of major energy sector asset owners (e.g., electric and gas utilities, petroleum companies) to proactively understand the state of security. Customized services include cybersecurity assessments, network architecture reviews, network scanning to look for static indicators and indicators of adversary persistence and anomalies, and control systems network traffic visualization.

Our I&A colleagues have increased outreach to the Energy Sector, providing expertise on malicious capabilities and intentions of emerging cyber threat actors targeting the sector, including in Unclassified forums. I&A leveraged partnerships with DHS and other Federal experts, including colleagues at DOE, to provide threat briefings to CEOs, CIOs, CISOs, and other private and public-sector leaders. These included engagements with the leadership and members of the American Petroleum Institute, alongside NPPD partners and National Security Staff colleagues, and a joint briefing with the FBI to the Federal Energy Regulatory Commission.

*Financial Sector Distributed Denial of Service (DDoS) Attacks*

The continued stability of the U.S. financial sector is often discussed as an area of concern, as U.S. banks are consistent targets of cyber attacks. DDoS incidents impacting leading U.S. banking institutions in 2012 and 2013 and periodically in 2014 have gotten more powerful as the DDoS campaign has persisted. US–CERT has a distinct role in responding to a DDoS: To disseminate victim notifications to United States Federal Agencies, Critical Infrastructure Partners, International CERTs, and U.S.-based Internet Service Providers.

US–CERT has provided technical data and assistance, including identifying 600,000 DDoS-related IP addresses and supporting contextual information in order to help financial institutions and their information technology security service providers improve their defensive capabilities. In addition to sharing with the relevant private-sector entities, US–CERT has provided this information to over 120 international partners, many of whom have contributed to our mitigation efforts. US–CERT, along with the FBI and other interagency partners, has also deployed on-site technical assistance to provide in-person support. US–CERT works with Federal civilian agencies to ensure that no U.S. Government systems are infected with botnet software that launches DDoS attacks and to increase the U.S. Government's domestic and international sharing and coordination efforts with public and private-sector partners.

During these attacks, our I&A partners bolstered long-term and consistent threat engagements with the Department of Treasury and private-sector partners throughout the Financial Services Sector. I&A analysts presented numerous sector-specific Unclassified briefings on the relevant threat intelligence, including at the annual FS–ISAC conference, alongside the Office of the National Counterintelligence Executive and the U.S. Secret Service. Additionally, at the request of the Treasury and the Financial and Banking Information Infrastructure Committee (FBIIC), I&A analysts provided Classified briefings on the malicious cyber threat actors to cleared individuals and groups from several financial regulators, including the Federal Deposit Insurance Corporation (FDIC), Securities and Exchange Commission (SEC), and the Federal Reserve Board (FRB).

## CONCLUSION

DHS is committed to creating a safe, secure, and resilient cyber environment while promoting cybersecurity knowledge and innovation and protecting confidentiality, privacy, and civil liberties in collaboration with our public, private, and international partners. We work around the clock to ensure that the peace and security of the American way of life will not be interrupted by opportunist enemies or terrorist actors. Each incarnation of threat has some unique traits. Mitigation requires agility and adaptation. Cybersecurity is not an end-state, but a continuous process of risk management.

We continue to believe that carefully-crafted information-sharing provisions, as part of a comprehensive suite of cybersecurity legislation, are essential to improving the Nation's cybersecurity, and we will continue to work with Congress and the White House to achieve this objective. We continue to seek legislation that clarifies and strengthens DHS responsibilities and allows us to respond quickly to vulnerabilities like Heartbleed. We continue to seek legislation that incorporates privacy, civil liberties, and confidentiality safeguards into all aspects of cybersecurity; strengthens our critical infrastructure's cybersecurity by further increasing information sharing and promoting the adoption of cybersecurity standards and guidelines; gives law enforcement additional tools to fight crime in the digital age; and creates a National Data Breach Reporting requirement.

DHS plays an integral role in promoting National cybersecurity: We are building a foundation of voluntary partnerships with private owners of critical infrastructure and Government partners working together to safeguard stability. We form a crucial underpinning for ensuring the on-going continuation of services. We work through information sharing, threat and indicator technical tools, sector-specific outreach, on-site technical assistance, education and awareness campaigns, and other mechanisms—in other words, we use a multi-dimensional approach that provides layered security. We look forward to continuing the conversation and continuing to serve the American goals of peace and stability, and we hope for your continued support.

Mr. KING. Thank you, Mr. Zelvin.

Now I would recognize Ms. Clarke for opening remarks.

Ms. CLARKE. I thank you, Mr. Chairman, and I thank Chairman Meehan and Ranking Member Higgins, for holding this hearing this morning.

As we have just heard and are keenly aware, threats to systems supporting U.S. critical infrastructure and Federal and corporate information systems are evolving and growing. Advanced persistent threats where adversaries possess sophisticated levels of expertise and significance pose increasing threats.

Soon after his election in 2008, President Obama declared the cyber threat to be one of the most serious economic and National security challenges we face as a Nation and stated America's economic prosperity in the 21st Century will depend on cybersecurity. The Director of National Intelligence has also warned us of the increasing globalization of cyber attacks, including those carried out by foreign militaries or organized international crime.

As has been mentioned already this morning, on Monday we saw the Department of Justice indict members of a foreign military involved in economic espionage cyber crime, most likely espionage in support of its state-owned companies. It appears that the Department of Justice has been working on this indictment for more than a year. Prosecutors in the DOJ's National Security Division had to show there was strong specific evidence, and there had to be companies that were willing to go public against China.

The evolving array of cyber-based threats facing the Nation pose threats to National security, commerce, and intellectual property, as well as individuals. International threats include both targeted and untargeted attacks from a variety of sources. These sources include business competitors, criminal groups, hackers, and foreign nations engaged in espionage and information warfare.

These sources of cybersecurity threats make use of various techniques to compromise information or adversely affect computers, software, a network or organization's operation and industry, or the internet itself. Such threat sources vary in terms of the types and capabilities of the actors, their willingness to act, and their motives. Adversarial cybersecurity threats can range from, as I like to say, from botnets to business competitors.

Addressing international cybersecurity threats involves many Government and private entities, including internet service providers, security vendors, software developers, and computer forensic specialists. Their focus is on developing and implementing technology systems to protect against computer intrusions, internet fraud and spam, and if a crime does occur, detecting it and helping to gather evidence for an investigation. Also, because cyber crime threats cross National and State borders, law enforcement organizations have to deal with multiple jurisdictions with their own laws and legal procedures, a situation that complicates and hobbles investigations.

Law enforcement's challenge in investigating and prosecuting malicious 21st Century cyber criminals is this: Modern criminals can readily leverage technology to victimize targets across borders, and the criminals themselves need not cross a single border to do so. This creates a unique test in identifying and locating the criminals and in apprehending and prosecuting them.

The United States has extradition treaties and mutual legal assistance agreements with some, but not all countries, and even with these agreements in place, the process may be slow. We must continue to search for ways that Congress can help enhance international law enforcement capabilities and to get criminals off the streets or, shall we say, out of cyberspace, and thus protect U.S. critical infrastructure, Government systems, and consumers.

I appreciate hearing the informed testimony of our witnesses this morning. It is reassuring to know that our Nation benefits from your diligence, knowledge, and expertise.

With that, Mr. Chairman, I yield back.

[The statement of Ms. Clarke follows:]

STATEMENT OF RANKING MEMBER YVETTE D. CLARKE

MAY 21, 2014

We all know that threats to systems supporting U.S. critical infrastructure, and Federal and corporate information systems are evolving and growing. Advanced persistent threats—where adversaries possess sophisticated levels of expertise and significant—pose increasing risks.

Soon after his election in 2008, President Obama declared the cyber threat to be "one of the most serious economic and National security challenges we face as a Nation" and stated "America's economic prosperity in the 21st Century will depend on cybersecurity." The Director of National Intelligence has also warned of the increasing globalization of cyber attacks, including those carried out by foreign militaries or organized international crime.

On Monday, we saw the Department of Justice indict members of a foreign military involved in economic espionage cyber crime, most likely espionage in support of its state-owned companies. It appears that the Department of Justice has been working on this indictment for more than a year. Prosecutors in the DOJ's National Security Division had to show there was strong, specific evidence, and there had to be companies that were willing to go public against China.

The evolving array of cyber-based threats facing the Nation poses threats to National security, commerce and intellectual property, and individuals. Intentional threats include both targeted and untargeted attacks from a variety of sources. These sources include business competitors, criminal groups, hackers, and foreign nations engaged in espionage and information warfare.

These sources of cybersecurity threats make use of various techniques to compromise information or adversely affect computers, software, a network, an organization's operation, an industry, or the internet itself. Such threat sources vary in terms of the types and capabilities of the actors, their willingness to act, and their motives. Adversarial cybersecurity threats can range from, as I like to say, "From Botnets to Business Competitors".

Addressing international cyber crime threats involves many Government and private entities—including internet service providers, security vendors, software developers, and computer forensics specialists. Their focus is on developing and implementing technology systems to protect against computer intrusions, internet fraud, and spam and, if a crime does occur, detecting it and helping to gather evidence for an investigation.

Also, because cyber crime threats cross National and State borders, law enforcement organizations have to deal with multiple jurisdictions with their own laws and legal procedures, a situation that complicates and hobbles investigations. Law enforcement's challenge in investigating and prosecuting malicious, 21st Century cybercriminals is this—modern criminals can readily leverage technology to victimize targets across borders, and the criminals themselves need not cross a single border to do so.

This creates a unique test in identifying and locating the criminals, and in apprehending and prosecuting them. The United States has extradition treaties and mutual legal assistance agreements with some, but not all countries. Even with these agreements in place, the process may be slow.

We must continue to search for ways that Congress can help enhance international law enforcement capabilities and to get criminals off the streets, or shall we say, out of cyberspace, and thus protect U.S. critical infrastructure, Government systems, companies, and consumers.

Mr. KING. I thank Ranking Member Clarke.

Now we will open up the hearing for a few questions. I just want to remind Members, however, that we are going to be moving to a closed session where these questions can be better addressed. But, again, if we can keep it to a few questions, I think it will be to everyone's benefit because there is much to be learned in closed session.

I just basically have one question, and I would ask it to the panel. Are terrorist organizations actively targeting the United States and have you seen cases of terror groups coordinating with criminal organizations to carry out attacks or to gain capability? Again we are in an open session, so you can tailor your answer accordingly.

Mr. DEMAREST. Yes, Chairman. So for this session, sir, yes, we are seeing that, but it is focused against the websites that are hosted in the United States, and they tend to be low-level attacks, website defacements and the like, maybe some DDoS activity. There are three principal groups that have the capabilities or are developing the capabilities today or are looking for the capabilities today to do something more I will say in the physical realm.

As far as your second part of the question about joining with criminal organizations, we have not seen that yet, though we do actively watch for terrorist organizations crossing over to the criminal forums that are on-line today to acquire a skill or talent or tools to perpetrate some greater crime.

Mr. KING. Do you believe that we have the defense capability? I know you said you want to head them off, but also do we have the defense capability against these type attacks?

Mr. DEMAREST. I think it is sector by sector, Chairman. I think in the dot-gov space we are fairly well-prepared, along with the dot-mil, but once you get into the dot-com space it is varying degrees of preparedness I would say, and I would probably defer to Larry on that, or Mr. Zelvin, as far as the sectors and how well they are prepared. But we see finance in particular doing a stellar job. They have invested heavily. Transportation and some of the others, energy. Then as you get down lower on the priority scale, less so.

Mr. KING. Mr. Lemons, Mr. Zelvin, any comment?

Mr. LEMONS. I would say I concur with Mr. Demarest at this point.

Mr. ZELVIN. Mr. Chairman, the only thing I think I would add is just that obviously law enforcement intelligence is doing their collection. Where we see this is reporting from victims, and then we turn it over to the FBI and other law enforcement both at the State and local level.

You know, most of the terrorist groups, especially domestic, are going after faith-based groups, so that has been mostly trying to influence and having an impact with those groups. We are working with them. Many of these groups don't have very sophisticated cyber defenses. So we are working with them not only to understand what may be targeting them, but also what companies out there can assist, and then obviously we offer assistance as well. I can cover more in the closed session if you like.

Mr. KING. Thank you.

Ranking Member Higgins.

Mr. HIGGINS. Thank you, Mr. Chairman.

It seems as though capability and desire are hard things to monitor and to detect, and it seems as though the cyber threat is coming from both state and non-state actors. So I would be interested in your assessment as to the terrorist threat from non-state actors like Hezbollah, Syria, and al-Qaeda. Terrorists second generation, post-9/11, are younger, more aggressive, and more technologically savvy. So I am just interested in your assessment of that relative to capability and desire to strike U.S. targets.

Mr. DEMAREST. Ranking Member, I would say the desire is strong. I will say the capability is developing. What we have seen among the three groups you mentioned, Lebanese Hezbollah is certainly an organization that is looking to develop a significant capability in this arena. They focus primarily on regional enemies, I will say their enemies, but not so much against the United States.

Mr. ZELVIN. Sir, I would concur with Mr. Demarest.

Mr. LEMONS. Me also, sir.

Mr. HIGGINS. What about the threat posed by state actors like Iran, China, and Russia? Is the level of activity increasing, and what are we doing to combat that?

Mr. DEMAREST. I will say certainly more for the closed session, sir, but significantly increasing on all three. I would say Russia, China, and Iran are certainly developing significant capabilities.

Mr. LEMONS. I would also concur with Mr. Demarest. As we see these nations also increase in complexity, their information needs also increase. Part of those information needs are also developing a cyber program to meet those needs as they go forward. We will get into more detail in the closed session, sir.

Mr. HIGGINS. I would just say in closing, the terrorist mentality is to target high-impact targets obviously, and 9/11, in addition to the death and destruction that was exacted on the United States, there was also a symbolic attack as well, which the cyber threat seems to confirm, and that is to disrupt our way of life. They attacked the Twin Towers because it was a sign of America's economic superiority. They attacked the Pentagon because it was a symbol of America's military superiority. Presumably a plane was headed for either the Capitol or the White House because of our democratic freedoms that we enjoy.

So it would seem to me that the potential of cyber attacks and the motivation and desire of those who seek to hurt us and our way of lives is pretty imminent and pretty significant. So I will yield back.

Mr. KING. Chairman Meehan.

Mr. MEEHAN. I thank you, Chairman King.

I thank, again, the panel for your work in this area.

We have looked at a variety of issues, and a lot of the focus continues to be, appropriately so, on the nation-state activity and the very sophisticated criminal gangs and the potential for them to do massive disruption, not only to our infrastructure, but also theft of intellectual property and things of that nature.

But Special Agent Demarest, you used a term, and it struck me, because you talked about this kind of a threat affecting not just our nations, but also our neighborhoods. I often think about the average American thinking about us discussing these issues and believing that somehow it is very remote from them—something might happen to some bank in New York, but it doesn't affect me. I praise law enforcement across the board, including the great work done by the Justice Department taking on sophisticated Chinese operations that have been sponsored, nation-sponsored activity, hacking into our most sophisticated systems.

But in your testimony you also talked about this process Blackshades, and in effect this is a market that exists out there in the world, you touched 19 countries with this very important indictment. Effectively, Blackshades, for anywhere between $5 and $40, individuals can go into the black market and purchase malware that if they are sophisticated enough, effectively they could go into the home of any American and take over their computer. As I understand your testimony, it is not only the ability to use that malware if it is invited in, in some capacity to take over the operation of a computer, including tracking the key strokes and things of that nature, but in reading the publicly-available information. So I am not talking about anything that hasn't been spoken about publicly.

Is it not accurate that in addition there was the capacity to be able to manipulate remotely the same kind of control functions that the individual would, including the use of cameras? So the reality is an individual could be sitting in their own home, they could be sitting in their own bedroom, and a remotely-controlled access would be able to not only have access to what is contained within their computer, but maybe actually in real time be actually viewing what is going on in that home. So we are inviting into our own homes, an average American, for as little as $5 some criminal in Eastern Europe or across the street would be able to have that access.

So I don't think we talk enough about this. Could you explain to me just what is Remote Access Tool? How is it available? What can it do? What are we doing to be able to take steps to prevent its use?

Mr. DEMAREST. Chairman Meehan, you are exactly right. You can imagine as a citizen sitting anywhere in the United States today, you could have an actor sitting in some remote region of the world actually viewing you through your own laptop or a computer at home through your camera.

Basically Remote Access Tool provides access by an actor to your box or to your computer to take it over. They own your PC or laptop or device that you are using. It gives them access, as you mentioned, to the web cam or the camera, and they can turn it on and off at will. As I mentioned, ransomware, they can lock files, take photos, whether they be sensitive photos to the individual, the owner of the computer or not, they collect all this information, financial information, passwords and the like. So it is completely owned. Then the information is taken and either used by that particular actor or sold in different environments on-line in these criminal forums.

So you are being exposed and exploited once, and then potentially multiple times by other actors who purchase the information on-line. Separately more, I guess, salt to the wound, they have the ability to send out chat messages to your contacts within your computer, so it looks like Chairman Meehan is sending Joe Demarest an email or chat and I respond to that. In that is a link that has the malware that is attached, so it then spreads the Blackshades now to my computer.

Mr. MEEHAN. So a friend could pick up what I think is a message to me that would just be in the normal course, I respond and send back a picture of our vacation that we took down to the Jersey shore, but because of that communication they now have access into my computer and now they can begin to do the same process, not only the taking over of the files and the key strokes, but potentially even manipulating the camera in my bedroom?

Mr. DEMAREST. Friends and family. What it would require from me when you send or after sending that chat to me, for me to click on a link that you send me via the chat message.

Mr. MEEHAN. How do we identify something like that in our system and what are we doing to be able to educate Americans to take steps to protect their most intimate and most private and most secure information, that which they do in the comfort of their own home?

Mr. DEMAREST. Excellent question. So throughout the investigation and in the culmination of the enforcement is a significant technical aspect to it where we are seizing the infrastructure used by the actors. Specifically, administrative servers, which has most of the victim information on it. So then we work with the victim, I will say the internet service providers for the various countries, to identify the victims and to get information to them, the fact that they have been impacted, and tools made available for them to actually mitigate or remediate what is on their computer. That again is the relationship we have forged with DHS, as offering through the DHS portal, but either tools or instructions on how to actually eliminate a given malware.

Mr. MEEHAN. Well, I will look forward to more communication with this as we go into private session and otherwise. But I thank all of you for your work. I think it is very important for the American people to recognize these issues and don't think of them always as just remotely affecting just big businesses or corporations, that everyday Americans, as you said, affecting not just our Nation, but our neighborhoods. I think this is part of our responsibility, is to open up an awareness and appreciation for the very scope and nature of this threat.

Thank you for your testimony. Look forward to hearing more at a later time. Yield back.

Mr. KING. Thank you, Chairman Meehan.

Ranking Member Clarke.

Ms. CLARKE. Thank you, Mr. Chairman.

Monday's indictment of the five Chinese military hackers for computer hacking and economic espionage was the sort of legal action taken by the AG as a standard tactic in espionage. It sends a clear signal to the other side that their actions have become intolerable. But it is just the beginning of a long process. The indictment alleged that the defendants conspired to hack into American computer systems, maintain authorized access, stealing information to advantage economic competitors in China.

As I understand, the Department of Homeland Security's role in these types of situations is usually led by US–CERT because it leads mitigation and forensic efforts in coordination with the FBI, Secret Service, and other Federal agencies. Would you describe the kind of interagency coordination that is in place for agencies as a collaborative model where DHS' involvement is stood up through US–CERT, and does the role go beyond that jurisdiction?

Mr. ZELVIN. Ranking Member, thank you for the question. So let me talk about it in broad terms, and we can get into more narrow as you like.

When there is an incident now we have a ranking system as to the importance of it. There are certain things that are low threshold and certain things are high threshold. It is a high threshold if somebody is into a database system. If there is a compromise of personal identifiable information, if there is a disruption or a destruction event, those are obviously very high-scale events. Fortunately they don't happen often, but they do happen.

On a given day we see between 150 and 200 incidents through our EINSTEIN system, which is monitoring the dot-gov through intrusion detection and intrusion prevention. At the high level we will make an outreach directly to the victim, and we will notify them of the event and making sure that they are tracking. Then we will offer assistance, if needed, to actually go and investigate on their servers and other information technology capabilities to determine how deep is the compromise.

We will do this in full partnership with the FBI, which will be leading law enforcement and domestic intelligence collection, we will do this with our own intelligence community members so they can develop the tactics, techniques, and procedures to see where else. Then US–CERT will go across the Federal community and create that awareness.

At the same time, we are creating signatures into the intrusion detection system to make sure that these events cannot be repeated, and then we are sharing it with the private and international partners through the Enhanced Cybersecurity Services or ECS, and also through our CISP program. So it is interagency, it is private sector, it is international, and even on the lower events we are still doing the notification. So I described the high end as more of an example. Then I would ask, see if Mr. Demarest wants to offer some thoughts as well.

Mr. DEMAREST. Madam Clarke, so what is great about today is that what Mr. Zelvin and the NCCIC in DHS learns informs the investigation, and what we learn through the investigation or intelligence collection efforts inform the protectors or the defenders, DHS. This is a cycle that has developed mightily, I will say, over the past 2 years where it this effective transfer of knowledge and information that better safeguards the country, but then informs and helps us spearhead and focus, finely focus investigations.

Ms. CLARKE. Very well. That is a very robust and holistic approach, and I think that that will serve our Nation well.

My next question is the debate around protecting U.S. networks is often focused on U.S. critical infrastructure. Currently the Department of Homeland Security from Presidential Policy Directive 21 lists 16 critical infrastructure sectors. Which of these sectors are targeted with probes and intrusions most frequently and what sectors are most at risk?

Mr. ZELVIN. Ranking Member, it really depends on the awareness. I will tell you, our energy sector, our finance sector, information technology, communications, transportation, we are seeing a lot of instances. There are other sectors that I haven't mentioned where we are not seeing it, but I wonder if that is because they are not being reported, and that is a huge challenge. When it comes to the critical infrastructure in the private sector, there is no requirement, it is all voluntary, so we know what we know, we don't know what we don't know, and I really worry about what we don't know.

So I have talked to groups and other sectors, and they said, we really don't have a cybersecurity problem. I said, oh, my gosh, yes, you do, you just don't know about it.

I will tell you my experience, and I think Mr. Lemons and Mr. Demarest will tell you the same thing. Adversaries are going after any vulnerability they can find. So it doesn't matter what State you are in, what city you are in, what critical infrastructure you are in, if there is an opening, there is an adversary that is going to see where they can go and what information they can steal.

Mr. DEMAREST. I would agree with Mr. Zelvin. Depending on the actor sometimes alters the focus or the most threatened sector. We talked about our Middle East actor in recent DDoS activity against New York over the past year or so. But again I think it depends on them, but I think Larry has mentioned the priority sectors for us today are finance, transportation, energy, IT, or communications.

Mr. LEMONS. Ranking Member, I think to the point from Mr. Zelvin and Mr. Demarest also, as we increase our outreach efforts within the private sector and our State and local partners, we see an increased willingness of people to come forward and work with us. So I believe that number continues to go higher and higher as we work with public and private partners.

Mr. KING. Thank the Ranking Member.

The gentleman from Georgia, Mr. Broun.

Mr. BROUN. Thank you, Mr. Chairman.

When CISPA was passed—several times now—a lot of people that are concerned about privacy and civil liberties all across the Nation were very fearful of that act because of the potential sharing of their own personal private information with the Federal Government. Can you tell me how that kind of information is being protected or is there any protection on people's privacy or civil liberties under CISPA?

Mr. ZELVIN. Congressman, at the forefront of everything we do is the protection of people's identifiable information, privacy, and civil liberties. It is an hourly, daily focus for us. I will tell you, my folks are trained on a routine basis, we are audited not only internally but also externally as far as our processes and procedures on how are we protecting that data.

We don't require that as cyber defenders, and that is what we do at DHS, at least in the NCCIC, we do not require information that is privacy, civil liberties in nature. The defense mechanisms are really those 1's and 0's from an attacking IT or malicious software.

I will tell you there have been instances, although rare, and also small, where we will get something from something that we thought was completely secure, and then we stop everything we do, and we go through a process with attorneys, with privacy experts, with civil liberties experts and making sure that if there is an incursion that we are treating it properly, that there is an ability to mitigate and to make sure that the spill doesn't go beyond what we have already detected, and then, as I said, go through the process and procedures and see where we may have failed that may have led to that. But as I said, that is a very rare occasion.

Mr. BROUN. So there is no guarantee, though, that privacy information is not shared either direction, from the company to the Federal Government or the Federal Government to other entities?

Mr. ZELVIN. Congressman, despite our best efforts and every process and procedure we have, there will be occasions where I regret there may be times where there may be spills, where that goes over. I think what is important is that we have the right processes, procedures, and oversight to make sure that when those occasions occur that we do the right things in accordance with the law, policy, and directives.

Mr. BROUN. Mr. Chairman, I will wait until the closed session for further questions.

Mr. KING. Okay. In accordance with the unanimous consent request at the beginning of the hearing, we will now recess the hearing and reconvene in 10 minutes for closed session in HVC–302. I would ask the audience if they would just wait and allow the witnesses to leave so we can take them to the location.

We stand in recess.

[Whereupon, at 11:00 a.m., the subcommittees proceeded in closed session and were subsequently adjourned at 12:18 p.m.]

○